Car Wonders

Amazing Facts and Stories About Cars

1

The first car was invented in 1886 by Karl Benz, a German engineer, and entrepreneur.

This car is widely regarded as the first practical automobile powered by an internal combustion engine. This car, the Benz Patent-Motorwagen, was a three-wheeled vehicle powered by a single-cylinder gasoline engine. The vehicle was able to reach a top speed of around 10 miles per hour and was patented in 1886.

2

The first automobile accident occurred in 1891 in Ohio, United States. The accident involved two cars, and no one was seriously injured.

3

The world's first car race was held in France in 1895. The race covered a distance of 732 miles (1,178 km) from Paris to Bordeaux and back.

4

The fastest car in the world is the Bugatti Chiron Super Sport 300+, which has a top speed of 304 mph (490 km/h). The car is powered by an 8.0-liter quad-turbocharged W16 engine that produces 1578 horsepower and 1180 lb-ft of torque!

5

The world's most expensive production car is the Bugatti La Voiture Noire, which was sold for $19 million in 2019.
The car is a one-of-a-kind model and was unveiled at the Geneva Motor Show in March 2019.

6

The average car has around 30,000 parts. These parts range from the engine and transmission to smaller components such as nuts, bolts, and screws.

7

The Lamborghini Aventador has a top speed of 217 mph (350 km/h) and can go from 0-60 mph in just 2.9 seconds.

The Lamborghini Aventador features a sleek and aerodynamic design, with a carbon fiber monocoque chassis and advanced suspension and braking systems, all of which contribute to its impressive performance capabilities.

8

By SenseiAlan

The first car radio was invented in 1929 by Paul Galvin, the founder of Motorola. The radio was called the "Motorola" and cost $130, which was a lot of money at the time.

The radio was a significant innovation in car technology and allowed drivers and passengers to listen to music, news, and other programming while on the road.

9

The first road trip in a car was completed by Bertha Benz, the wife of Karl Benz, in 1888. She drove a Benz Patent-Motorwagen from Mannheim to Pforzheim, a distance of around 66 miles (106 km), with her two sons to demonstrate the car's capabilities and generate publicity for her husband's invention.

10

The world's first electric traffic signal was installed in Cleveland, Ohio, in 1914. The traffic signal was invented by James Hoge, a police officer in Salt Lake City, Utah, who had grown frustrated with the chaos and danger of manually-operated traffic signals. The first electric traffic signal was installed at the intersection of Euclid Avenue and East 105th Street in Cleveland, Ohio, and was operated manually by a police officer who controlled the lights using a switch.

11

The first car to have seat belts as a standard feature was the 1958 Saab GT750. Saab, a Swedish car manufacturer, made safety a top priority and introduced the seat belt as a standard feature in the GT750 model. However, Volvo is still widely credited with popularizing the three-point safety belt, which was invented by Nils Bohlin, a Volvo engineer, in 1959. The three-point safety was eventually adopted by other automakers around the world and now is considered one of the most important safety innovations in the history of the automobile.

12

The largest car manufacturer in the world is currently Toyota, which produces over 10 million vehicles per year and has a market capitalization of over $200 billion!

13

The first car with an automatic transmission was the 1940 Oldsmobile, which featured a new transmission system called the Hydra-Matic. The Hydra-Matic was developed by General Motors and was the first automatic transmission to be used in a mass-produced car. Prior to the introduction of the Hydra-Matic, all cars had manual transmissions that required drivers to shift gears manually using a clutch and a gearshift. The Hydra-Matic system, on the other hand, used a hydraulic torque converter to automatically shift gears, making driving easier and more convenient.

14

The first car with air conditioning was the 1939 Packard, which featured a system that blew air over a block of ice in the trunk.

15

The longest traffic jam on record occurred in China in 2010 and lasted for over 10 days! The jam stretched for more than 60 miles (97 km) and was caused by a combination of factors, including roadworks, bottlenecks, and heavy congestion on a major highway leading into Beijing.

16

The Volkswagen Beetle, one of the most iconic cars in history, was originally designed by Ferdinand Porsche for Adolf Hitler as a car for the people. In the 1930s, Hitler wanted to create a car that was affordable and accessible to the average German citizen (the term "Volkswagen" means "People's Car" in German). However, the outbreak of World War II delayed the production of the car, and it was not until after the war that it was finally mass-produced and marketed to the public.

The Ford Model T, also known as the "Tin Lizzie," was the first car to be mass-produced on an assembly line*, which revolutionized the automobile industry and made cars more affordable and accessible to the general public. The Model T was produced by the Ford Motor Company from 1908 to 1927, and during that time, more than 15 million Model Ts were produced. The car was designed to be simple and rugged, with interchangeable parts and a powerful engine that could run on gasoline or ethanol.

*Assembly line:
The assembly line method of production is a manufacturing process that involves dividing the production process into a series of tasks and having each worker specialize in one task. The product being manufactured moves along a conveyor belt or an assembly line, and each worker performs their task as the product passes by.

The Jensen FF (which stood for Ferguson Formula) was the first production car to feature a four-wheel drive system. The car was designed by the British car manufacturer Jensen Motors and introduced in 1966.

The four-wheel drive system used in the Jensen FF was developed by Harry Ferguson Research, which was also responsible for developing the four-wheel drive system used in Formula One racing cars. The system used a specially designed transfer box that allowed the power from the engine to be distributed evenly to all four wheels, improving traction and handling on both wet and dry roads. The Jensen FF was powered by a 6.3-liter V8 engine and featured other advanced technologies for its time, including an anti-lock braking system* (ABS) and traction control*. The car was also equipped with a luxurious interior and had a top speed of 131 mph (211 km/h).

*Anti-lock Braking System (ABS):

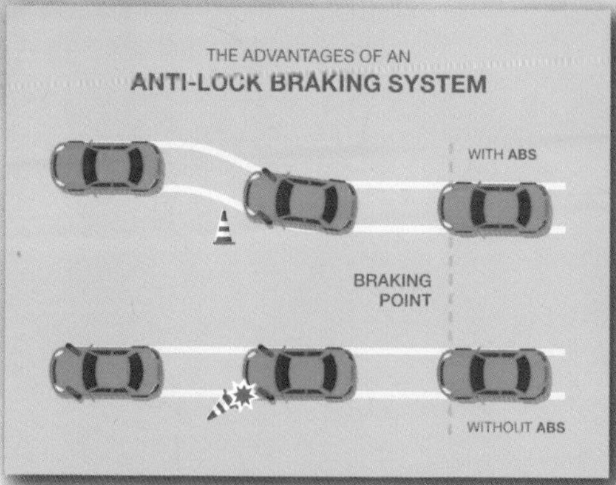

An Anti-lock Braking System (ABS) is a safety feature that prevents the wheels of a vehicle from locking up during hard braking, helping the driver to keep steering and to keep control of the vehicle and avoid accidents.

ABS uses sensors on each wheel to monitor its speed, and when the system detects that one or more wheels are about to lock up, it momentarily releases the brake pressure on that wheel. By doing so, it allows the wheel to rotate and regain traction with the road surface, helping to prevent skidding and maintaining steering control.

ABS has become a standard safety feature in most modern vehicles, and it has been proven to significantly reduce the risk of accidents caused by loss of control during hard braking.

*Traction Control:

Traction control is a safety feature that helps to prevent the wheels of a vehicle from losing traction with the road surface during acceleration. It works by using sensors to monitor the speed of each wheel and detect when one or more of the wheels are slipping or losing traction. When this happens, the traction control system reduces engine power or applies the brakes to the wheel or wheels that are slipping, helping to redirect power to the wheels that have better traction.Traction control is particularly useful in slippery or low-grip conditions such as snow, ice, or wet roads, where wheels can easily lose traction and cause the vehicle to lose control.

19

Did you know that the 1984 Mercedes-Benz S-Class was the first car to have airbags as a standard safety feature? Airbags are like giant pillows that inflate during a crash to protect the driver and passengers from hitting the hard surfaces inside the car. They work together with seat belts to provide extra protection in case of a collision. Nowadays, airbags are common in almost all modern cars and are considered an essential safety feature.

20

The first speeding ticket was issued in 1902 in Dayton, Ohio, when a driver was caught going 12 miles per hour in a 10 mph zone.

This event marked the beginning of traffic enforcement in the United States.

21

The 1976 Cadillac Fleetwood 75 is the longest production car ever made, measuring over 23 feet long. To put that in perspective, that's longer than two average-sized cars parked end to end! This luxurious car was popular among politicians and celebrities, and it had plenty of legroom for even the tallest passengers. However, its size made it difficult to park and maneuver in tight spaces. Despite this, the Cadillac Fleetwood 75 remains an iconic symbol of American automotive engineering and luxury.

22

Limousines are typically longer than regular cars, but they are not usually considered as production cars because they are often custom-made or modified by aftermarket coachbuilders.

23

The first car to use a rearview mirror was the 1911 Marmon Wasp, which won the inaugural Indianapolis 500 race that year. The 1911 Marmon Wasp, driven by Ray Harroun, was equipped with a rearview mirror that allowed him to see the cars behind him without having to turn his head. This gave him an advantage in the race and helped him secure the victory. The rearview mirror later became a standard feature in cars and is still an important safety device today.

24

In 1938, Chevrolet introduced the first car with a trunk that could be opened remotely using a key fob, meaning that people could open their car trunks without using a key directly on the lock.

25

The world's smallest car is the Peel P50, a three-wheeled car that measures just 54 inches long and 41 inches wide. The Peel P50 is so small that it can be driven through a standard doorway! It was originally designed as a city car in the 1960s and only about 50 were ever made. Today, it is considered a collector's item and has been featured in several movies and TV shows. Despite its small size, the Peel P50 can still reach a top speed of 35 mph and has a fuel efficiency of around 100 miles per gallon. Despite it's size the original Peel P50 has always been road-legal in the UK!

26

The Oldsmobile Curved Dash was the first car to be produced in series in the United States. It was a popular car at the time and was produced from 1901 to 1907, with over 19,000 units sold during its production run.

27

In 2011, a man in Massachusetts accidentally parked his car on a beach and went for a walk. As the tide came in, the car got swept away and disappeared into the ocean. The man was able to recover the car a few days later, and incredibly, it still started and drove home. The car, a 1992 Buick Roadmaster, was later nicknamed the "Buick of the deep" and became somewhat of a local legend.

28

The first electric car was invented in the early 1800s, and many inventors and manufacturers continued to experiment with electric car designs throughout the 19th and early 20th centuries. However, the first practical electric car that was widely produced and sold to consumers was the 1901 La Jamais Contente, a Belgian car that was designed by Camille Jenatzy and powered by batteries.

The McLaren F1 was the first car to use a carbon fiber* monocoque chassis, which made it both strong and lightweight. The McLaren F1, which was produced from 1992 to 1998, was a groundbreaking sports car in many ways, it was powered by a BMW-built V12 engine that produced over 600 horsepower, and it was capable of reaching a top speed of over 240 miles per hour. Only 106 examples of the F1 were ever built, making it a highly sought-after and collectible sports car.

*Carbon fiber is a lightweight and strong material made from thin fibers of carbon, typically woven together into a fabric-like texture. The fibers are then combined with a resin material to create a composite material that is both strong and lightweight. Carbon fiber is known for its excellent strength-to-weight ratio, making it a popular material for use in high-performance sports cars, airplanes, and other applications where weight reduction is important. Carbon fiber is more expensive than traditional materials like steel or aluminum, but its high performance and durability make it a popular choice for many applications.

30

The Dodge Viper was originally designed as a concept car, but it was so popular that it went into production in 1992. The concept car was unveiled at the North American International Auto Show in Detroit in 1989, and due to the overwhelming interest in the concept car, Chrysler decided to put the Viper into production. The first generation of the Viper, also known as the RT/10, was produced from 1992 to 1995. The Viper has since become a popular and iconic American sports car, with several generations and variants produced over the years.

31

In some countries, such as Japan, it is customary for limousines to have a white exterior and a red interior.

32

The Queen of England has several Rolls-Royce limousines in her fleet, which are used for state occasions.

33

Limousines were originally designed as chauffeur-driven cars for the wealthy in the early 20th century.
Limousines were longer and more spacious than regular cars, and they often featured amenities such as leather seats, air conditioning, and built-in bars. Today, limousines are still associated with luxury and prestige, and they are often used for special occasions such as weddings, proms, and business events.

34

The word "limousine" comes from the French region of Limousin, where the shepherds wore a type of hood that looked similar to the roof of a limousine.

35

The "American Dream" limousine is a custom-built limousine that has held the Guinness World Record for the longest car in the world at 100 feet long. It was built by designer and builder Jay Ohrberg in California in the 1990s and features a variety of unique amenities such as a swimming pool with a diving board, a helipad, a king-size water bed, a sun deck, a Jacuzzi, and even a satellite dish. The limousine was also featured in several movies and television shows, including "Batman Returns" and "Mystery Men".

36

The most expensive limousine in the world is the $4.8 million "Midnight Rider" limousine, which features a fireplace, a king-size bed, and a 40-inch plasma TV. It was custom-built for an anonymous client in the United States.

37

The largest limousine fleet in the world is operated by the Las Vegas-based company, Presidential Limousine.

Presidential Limousine is a well-known luxury transportation company that provides limousine services for various events such as weddings, corporate events, and airport transportation.

38 In 1964, a man named Bob Kearns came up with the idea of intermittent windshield wipers while driving his car in the rain. He developed a prototype and began pitching it to automakers, but they all rejected his idea. Kearns refused to give up, and he eventually sued Ford and Chrysler for patent infringement, claiming that they had stolen his idea. The case went to trial, and Kearns ultimately won, receiving over $30 million in damages. His invention is now a standard feature on almost all cars.

39 The first sports car is widely considered to be the 1910 Prince Henry Vauxhall, which was built for a long-distance race and had a top speed of 60 mph.

Other early sports cars include the 1898 Mors 60 HP, the 1900 Lanchester 28 HP "Prince Henry," and the 1903 Mercedes-Simplex 60 hp

40

The Lamborghini Countach was designed to look like an "Italian wedge" and was one of the most popular sports cars of the 1980s. The Lamborghini Countach, designed by Marcello Gandini, was first introduced in 1974 and produced until 1990. Its distinctive wedge-shaped design with angular lines and scissor doors made it an iconic sports car of the 1980s. The Countach was powered by a V12 engine and had a top speed of over 180 mph, making it one of the fastest cars of its time.

41

The Porsche 911 is one of the most iconic sports cars in the world, and it has been in production since 1963. It is known for its distinctive design, performance, and handling, and has gone through several generations and updates throughout its history.

42 The Ford GT40 was designed specifically to beat Ferrari in the 24 Hours of Le Mans race, and it succeeded by winning the race four years in a row from 1966 to 1969. The GT40 was designed by a team of engineers led by Carroll Shelby and was powered by a 7.0-liter V8 engine. Its low, sleek design and powerful engine made it a formidable competitor on the track, and it remains an icon of automotive racing history.

43 The Bugatti Veyron is one of the most powerful and expensive supercars in the world, and it is capable of reaching speeds of over 250 miles per hour. However, during a test drive in 2007, a British journalist named Richard Hammond crashed a Veyron at a speed of 288 miles per hour, causing the car to burst into flames. Despite suffering serious injuries, Hammond survived the crash and later joked about it, saying that he had "turned a car into a firework".

44

Koenigsegg is a Swedish manufacturer of high-performance supercars known for their unique and innovative designs. The company was founded in 1994 by Christian von Koenigsegg when he was just 22 years old. Koenigsegg produces a limited number of cars each year, with the total production typically under 30 cars. The Koenigsegg Jesko has a top speed of over 300 mph, and is expected to break the speed record set by the Bugatti Chiron.

45

The Ferrari 458 Italia was named the "Best Driver's Car" by Motor Trend in 2011, thanks to its handling, performance, and design.

46 The Ferrari 250 GTO is one of the most valuable and sought-after classic cars in the world. Only 39 of these cars were built between 1962 and 1964, and they were designed specifically for racing. Today, they are considered a masterpiece of automotive engineering and design, and are highly prized by collectors. In 2018, a 1963 Ferrari 250 GTO was sold at auction for a record-breaking $70 million, making it the most expensive car ever sold. However, the average value of a Ferrari 250 GTO is around $48 million!

47 The Porsche 911 has been in continuous production since 1963, making it one of the longest-running sports car models in history.

48 The fastest production electric car is the Rimac C_Two, which has a top speed of 258 mph (415 km/h). The Rimac C_Two is an all-electric hypercar that is currently in production, and is expected to be released in limited numbers in 2023. It has four electric motors that produce a combined output of 1,914 horsepower, and can accelerate from 0 to 60 mph (97 km/h) in under 2 seconds.

49 The Aston Martin Valkyrie hypercar was designed by Formula 1 aerodynamicist Adrian Newey. It has a top speed of over 250 mph and can accelerate from 0 to 60 mph in less than 2.5 seconds. The Aston Martin Valkyrie is a limited-production car, with only 150 units planned for production.

50

The largest tire producer in the world is currently the Japanese company Bridgestone Corporation. The company produces a wide range of tires for cars, trucks, motorcycles, bicycles, and other vehicles, as well as rubber and other diversified products. Bridgestone operates in more than 150 countries and has more than 180 manufacturing plants worldwide. In 2020, the company produced more than 190 million tires. Other major tire manufacturers include Michelin, Goodyear, Continental, and Pirelli, among others.

51

The Mercedes-AMG One hypercar has a Formula 1-derived powertrain, with a turbocharged V6 engine and four electric motors, producing over 1,000 horsepower making it one of the most powerful road cars ever built!

52

The Chevrolet Corvette has been in production since 1953 and is one of the most popular sports cars in America.

It is widely regarded as one of the most iconic and popular sports cars in America, known for its sleek styling, high performance, and affordability. Despite its long history and popularity, the Corvette remains an accessible sports car that is relatively affordable compared to many of its competitors.

53

The Audi R8 was the first production car in the world to come equipped with full-LED headlights. This was a major technological advancement at the time, and helped to establish Audi as a leader in automotive lighting technology.

The Lamborghini Aventador SVJ has a Nurburgring* lap time of 6:44.97, making it one of the fastest production cars to ever lap the track. The Aventador SVJ is powered by a 6.5-liter V12 engine that produces over 750 horsepower, and it features a range of advanced aerodynamic technologies and performance-enhancing features that help it to achieve incredible speeds and handling capabilities.

*Nürburgring

The Nürburgring is a famous racetrack located in Nürburg, Germany. It is considered one of the most challenging and demanding racetracks in the world, with a length of over 20 kilometers (12.4 miles) and more than 170 corners. The track is often used for testing and development of high-performance sports cars, and many car manufacturers use their lap times around the track as a measure of their car's performance capabilities.

55

The Porsche 918 Spyder is the first production car to lap the Nurburgring in under seven minutes, with a time of 6:57.

the Porsche 918 Spyder is that it was actually designed as a concept car in 2010, and was initially not intended for production. However, the overwhelmingly positive reception convinced Porsche to develop the car for production.

56

The Ferrari SF90 Stradale is the first plug-in hybrid production car from Ferrari. It features a hybrid powertrain that combines a twin-turbocharged V8 engine with three electric motors, producing a total combined output of 986 horsepower.

57

The McLaren Senna is an incredibly aerodynamic sports car, designed to produce massive amounts of downforce to keep the car glued to the road at high speeds. At 155 mph, the Senna generates up to 1,764 pounds of downforce, which is more than the weight of the car itself! This is achieved through a combination of advanced aerodynamic features, including active aerodynamics, a massive rear wing, and a specially designed underbody that channels airflow to create downforce.

58

60 million cars are produced every year. That's 165,000 cars a day, 6,875 an hour and 115 a minute!

59

In 2021, there were around 1.4 billion cars in use worldwide. This number represents roughly one car for every seven people on Earth. However car ownership varies widely by country and region. Some countries have higher rates of car ownership than others, for example there is one car per person in the US including infants which means approximately 300 million cars.

60

Prince Charles has a car fuelled by wine. Prince Charles, the Prince of Wales, is known for his environmentally conscious lifestyle, and this extends to the vehicles he uses. It has been reported that he owns a car that runs on wine, specifically bioethanol derived from fermented wine. Bioethanol is a renewable fuel made from crops such as corn, sugarcane, or in this case, wine, and is considered a more environmentally friendly alternative to traditional fossil fuels.

61

• Volkswagen AG is a German multinational automotive company that owns a portfolio of well-known twelve brands from different European countries. These brands range from budget-friendly to luxury cars and include Volkswagen Passenger Cars, Audi, Seat, Skoda, Bentley, Bugatti, Lamborghini, Porsche, Ducati, Volkswagen Commercial Vehicles, Scania, and MAN.

62

The largest car speeding fine ever produced was in Switzerland, where a Swedish man was caught driving at 180 mph (290 km/h) in a Mercedes-Benz SLS AMG. He was fined €1,000,000 for the offense in 2010. The reason why the speeding ticket was so expensive is that, unlike in the United States, the amount of a speeding ticket fine in Switzerland is determined by a combination of a driver's income and the speed recorded.

63 The chance of dying in a car accident is approximately 1 in 5,000, which makes driving appear quite risky when compared to the odds of dying in a plane crash (1 in 11 million).

64 The record for the highest total mileage clocked by a single car belongs to a 1966 Volvo P1800, which has been owned by Irv Gordon since 1966. Gordon has driven the car more than 3 million miles, with the milestone being achieved in September 2013. The car's odometer famously rolled over the 1 million mile mark in 1987.

65 Ralph Teetor, the inventor of cruise control, was blind! He was inspired to create the technology after riding in a car with his lawyer. Teetor developed the first version of cruise control in the 1940s and patented the technology in 1950.

66

Airbags are designed to deploy rapidly in the event of a collision to help protect occupants from serious injuries. They typically deploy at speeds of up to 200 mph, or 322 km/h, and can inflate within 20 to 30 milliseconds of a collision. The deployment speed and force of the airbag are carefully controlled by sensors that detect the severity and angle of the impact, as well as the weight and position of the occupants.

67

According to the Texas A&M Transportation Institute, the average American driver spends around 20 hours per year waiting at red lights, which adds up to almost two weeks over the course of a lifetime.

68

• Every year, over $60 billion worth of car maintenance goes unperformed. This includes routine services such as oil changes, tire rotations, and other essential maintenance tasks. Failing to perform these services can lead to more significant problems down the road, resulting in expensive repairs and even unsafe driving conditions.

69

The most people ever to fit inside a Smart car is 19. The feat was accomplished by a group of gymnasts from the UK in September 2011, who managed to cram themselves into the tiny vehicle in front of a live audience.

70 Rolls-Royce is handmade! Rolls-Royce cars are known for their exquisite craftsmanship and attention to detail. Each car is built by hand by a team of highly skilled craftsmen and engineers, who use traditional techniques and the finest materials to create these luxurious vehicles. It takes over 800 hours to build a Rolls-Royce car, with many of the processes, such as painting, polishing, and leatherworking, completed by hand. The result is a car that is not only beautiful to look at but also a pleasure to drive. That's why Rolls-Royce cars are among the most expensive and luxurious vehicles in the world. The price range for a new Rolls-Royce car typically starts around $300,000 for the Rolls-Royce Ghost, and can go up to several millions of dollars for bespoke models, limited editions, or fully customized cars like the Rolls-Royce Sweptail.

Rolls-Royce Ghost

Rolls-Royce Sweptail

71

The Toyota Corolla is one of the most popular and best-selling cars in the world, with a history dating back to its launch in 1966. According to Toyota, the Corolla is sold in over 150 countries and regions, with an estimated 1 Corolla sold every 15 seconds. As of 2021, the company has sold more than 44.1 million Corolla cars worldwide, which accounts for roughly 20% of the company's overall sales. The Corolla is known for its reliability, fuel efficiency, and affordability, and has become a staple of the Toyota lineup over the years.

72

The Honda Accord has been named to Car and Driver magazine's 10 Best list a record 34 times, more than any other car in history. The Honda Accord is known for its reliability, practicality, and value, and has earned a reputation as one of the most dependable cars on the road.

73

According to data from used-car retailer CarMax, black was the best-selling car color in the United States in 2018, accounting for 22.3% of cars sold. White was the second most popular color at 19.3%, followed by gray (17.6%) and silver (14.6%). While car color preferences can vary by region and individual taste, these colors have remained some of the most popular choices among car buyers in recent years.

74

The automobile industry is a major contributor to the U.S. economy, employing millions of people across various sectors, including manufacturing, sales, marketing, and support services. According to the Auto Alliance, the automobile industry employs 9.9 million Americans, which accounts for about 5.1% of private-sector employment in the United States.

75

Driver distraction is a leading cause of car accidents, with up to 80% of crashes involving some form of distraction. On average, a crash occurs within three seconds of a driver becoming distracted.

76

The Ferrari 290 MM was a legendary race car produced by Ferrari in the 1950s. It was powered by a 3.5-liter V12 engine capable of producing 320 horsepower and was designed for endurance racing. The car won the prestigious Mille Miglia race in 1956, with Eugenio Castellotti at the wheel, who completed the grueling 1,000-mile race in under 11 hours, averaging a speed of over 97 miles per hour. Today, the Ferrari 290 MM is considered an icon in the world of motorsports and is highly coveted by collectors and enthusiasts.

77

The Bugatti Royale, also known as the Type 41, is a luxury car produced by Bugatti in the 1930s. It was designed to be the most luxurious and powerful car of its time, and only six were ever built. The car was powered by a massive 12.7-liter engine, which produced over 300 horsepower, making it one of the most powerful cars of its time. The Bugatti Royale was also one of the longest cars ever built, measuring over 21 feet in length, with a wheelbase of more than 14 feet. Today, the Bugatti Royale is considered one of the most iconic and rarest cars in the world, with one example selling for over $9 million at auction in 1987.

78

The average car spends about 95% of its time parked. This means that on average, a car is only in use for about 5% of the time it exists. This is one reason why car-sharing services and ride-sharing services have become more popular.

79 The Autobahn is considered one of the most famous highways in the world, and its high speeds and lack of speed limits have become a part of German culture. However, it is important to note that driving on the Autobahn requires a high level of skill and concentration, and accidents can still occur at high speeds. The first section of the Autobahn was built in 1921, and it has since grown to over 7,000 miles in length.

80 NASCAR was actually created because of Prohibition. During Prohibition in the US, moonshiners would transport their illegal alcohol across the country using fast cars that had been modified to outrun the police. These drivers would race each other in order to prove who had the fastest car. The first official NASCAR race was held in 1948 in Daytona Beach, Florida, and the sport has since become one of the most popular forms of motorsport in the world.

81

Ferrari's meticulous attention to detail ensures that when someone purchases a Ferrari, they are joining a highly exclusive club. With a production rate of no more than 14 cars per day, Ferrari's manufacturing process is significantly slower than that of other car manufacturers such as Toyota, which was able to produce up to 13,400 cars per day in 2014.

82

In 1905, brake lights were invented, replacing the need for drivers to use hand signals to indicate their stopping or slowing down. Before the introduction of brake lights, the use of hand signals was particularly challenging during nighttime when visibility was reduced. Nowadays, brake lights are a compulsory safety feature for all vehicles.

83

The Mercedes-Benz 300SLR was a racing car produced by Mercedes-Benz between 1955 and 1956. It was designed to compete in the World Sportscar Championship, and famously won the 1955 Mille Miglia race with driver Stirling Moss behind the wheel. The 300SLR had a lightweight body made of magnesium alloy, and was powered by a 3.0-liter straight-eight engine capable of producing up to 310 horsepower. Only nine 300SLR models were ever produced, and they are highly coveted by collectors, with one example selling for over $30 million in 2013.

84

Alcohol is a significant factor in approximately 50% of all fatal car accidents in the United States.

85 Many modern sports cars and supercars are equipped with speakers that emit an artificial engine sound, which is designed to enhance the driving experience and provide a more thrilling auditory experience for the driver and passengers. This technology is often used in electric and hybrid cars, which don't have the same level of engine noise as traditional gasoline-powered cars. The sound can be adjusted to the driver's preferences and can even mimic the sound of a traditional high-performance engine, despite the car's actual power source.

86 The automobile industry is one of the largest recyclers in the world. About 95% of a car's materials can be recycled, and the industry is continually working to increase that percentage. The recycling of cars, bikes, and trucks generates billions of dollars annually and creates jobs in the recycling and scrap industries.

87

The gullwing doors on the Mercedes-Benz SLS AMG add to its distinct appearance and were inspired by the iconic 1950s Mercedes-Benz 300SL "Gullwing" sports car. The SLS AMG was produced from 2010 to 2015 and was known for its powerful engine and luxurious features.

88

The Porsche Taycan is the first all-electric production car from Porsche, with a range of up to 300 miles (483 km) on a single charge. The Porsche Taycan was first introduced in 2019 and features impressive performance, with some models able to accelerate from 0 to 60 mph in under 3 seconds.

89

The Ferrari LaFerrari was the first hybrid car produced by Ferrari. It combines a 6.3-liter V12 engine with an electric motor, producing a total output of 950 horsepower. The car can go from 0 to 60 mph in less than 3 seconds and has a top speed of 217 mph. Only 499 units of the LaFerrari were produced, making it a highly exclusive and sought-after car among collectors.

90

A hypercar is a type of high-performance sports car that is designed for extreme speed and acceleration. It is typically more powerful and faster than a standard supercar, with advanced engineering and technology. Hypercars are often limited production vehicles with exclusive designs and features, and are usually very expensive.

91

The Bugatti Bolide was unveiled in 2020 by the French luxury car manufacturer Bugatti. It is a track-focused hypercar with a weight of just 1,240 kg, thanks to its extensive use of lightweight materials such as titanium and carbon fiber. The Bolide is powered by a quad-turbocharged 8.0-liter W16 engine that produces 1,825 horsepower, and it can reach a top speed of over 311 mph (500 km/h). The car's unique design includes an adjustable rear wing and a roof-mounted air scoop to increase downforce and improve aerodynamics. In August 2021, Bugatti announced that the production Bolide has its first delivery scheduled for 2024 and will be limited to 40 units. The net unit price is set at €4 million.

92

Hong Kong has one of the highest densities of Rolls Royce vehicles in the world. This is largely due to the city's high concentration of wealthy individuals and its luxury car culture.

93

The "new car smell" is actually a combination of many different organic compounds that are emitted by the various materials used in the car's interior, such as seat fabrics, plastics, and adhesives.
While many people enjoy the smell, it's worth noting that some of these compounds can be harmful in high concentrations, so it's important to ensure good ventilation when driving a new car.

94 The Lexus LFA has a unique engine note that was specifically tuned by Yamaha to sound like a Formula 1 car. Its engine is a V10 that was developed in partnership with Yamaha, and it produces a distinct exhaust note that has been compared to the sound of a Formula 1 car. The sound has become one of the defining features of the LFA and is highly sought after by car enthusiasts.

95

The first armored presidential car was a 1939 Cadillac Series 75 that was specially built for President Franklin D. Roosevelt. It had inch-thick windows, armor-plated doors, and a specially reinforced chassis to protect the president in case of an attack. This car was nicknamed "The Beast" and set the precedent for future presidential vehicles to have advanced security features.

96

The Thrust SSC (British SuperSonic jet-powered car) is the current world record holder for the fastest land speed car, achieving a top speed of 1,227.986 km/h (763.035 mph) on October 15, 1997, in the Black Rock Desert of Nevada, USA. The car was driven by Royal Air Force fighter pilot Andy Green.

97

According to a 2021 study by the transportation analytics firm INRIX, the average American driver spends 38 hours per year stuck in traffic congestion. This can vary by city, with some urban areas experiencing much higher levels of traffic congestion than others.

98

Surprisingly Elon Musk is not the founder of Tesla Motors. While Elon Musk is not the founder of Tesla Motors, he played a key role in the company's success and development. Tesla Motors was actually founded in 2003 by Martin Eberhard and

Marc Tarpenning. However, Musk became involved in the company shortly after its founding, investing a significant amount of his personal wealth into the company and taking over as CEO in 2008.

99

Sugarcane is one of the primary sources used to produce ethanol, a type of biofuel that can be used as an alternative to gasoline. In countries like Brazil, ethanol produced from sugarcane is widely used as a fuel for cars, and it is considered to be a renewable and environmentally friendly alternative to fossil fuels.

100 Women buy more new cars than men! According to a 2021 study by Cox Automotive, women accounted for 54% of new car purchases in the United States in 2020, while men accounted for 46%. This represents a significant shift from previous years, where men were more likely to purchase new cars than women.

101 Tesla electric cars offer the largest dashboard multimedia screen. Yes, there are a few physical buttons, but 95% of car features are controlled by a 12.3-inch LCD touch screen.

102 The first mass-produced off-road vehicle was the Willys Jeep, which was produced during World War II for use by the U.S. military.

BMW i8 is the world's first sports car to be developed with sustainability in mind, featuring a hybrid powertrain that combines a 1.5-liter three-cylinder gasoline engine with an electric motor and a lithium-ion battery pack for a total output of 369 horsepower. The car also has a lightweight carbon fiber and aluminum construction, which allows it to achieve a fuel economy rating of 76 MPGe (miles per gallon equivalent) and a zero-to-60-mph time of just 4.2 seconds. The i8 also features futuristic gull-wing doors and an aerodynamic design that helps it to cut through the air with minimal drag. The BMW i8 was also the first production car to feature laser headlights. The laser headlights offered significantly better visibility than traditional LED headlights and were more energy-efficient.

104

Formula 1 cars can accelerate from 0 to 60 mph in less than 2 seconds, making them the fastest accelerating cars in the world.

105

The Tesla Model S has a drag coefficient of 0.208, which is the lowest of any production car. The low drag coefficient helps the car achieve better efficiency and longer range on a single charge. The Tesla Model S was also the first electric car to receive the Motor Trend Car of the Year award in 2013, which was a significant milestone for electric cars.

106 In 1966, the US Congress passed the National Traffic and Motor Vehicle Safety Act, which created safety standards for cars, including seat belts, padded dashboards, and safety glass.

107 The first car to have a built-in GPS system was the Mazda Eunos Cosmo, which was introduced in Japan in 1990. At that time, the fourth generation of Mazda Eunos Cosmo was considered a technological marvel.

108 The BMW headquarters in Munich, Germany, is designed in the shape of four cylinders, which symbolizes the company's heritage in aircraft engine manufacturing.

109 Ferruccio Lamborghini, who was already a successful manufacturer of tractors, had owned several Ferraris, but he was not satisfied with the quality of the cars' clutches. When he approached Enzo Ferrari with his concerns, Ferrari dismissed him, saying that he was just a tractor maker and did not know anything about sports cars. This insult prompted Lamborghini to start his own line of high-performance sports cars, which quickly gained popularity for their sleek design and powerful engines. The first Lamborghini car, the 350 GTV, was unveiled at the Turin Motor Show in 1963, and the company continued to produce a series of successful models, including the Miura, Countach, and Diablo.

110

4

The first speed limit was introduced in the UK in 1865, and it was 4 mph in the country and 2 mph in the city!

111

In 2007, a man named Andy Saunders from the UK bought a vintage 1935 Aston Martin Ulster for £70,000 (approximately $96,000 at the time). However, when he took the car to be serviced, he discovered a hidden compartment that contained an extremely rare 1920s Leica camera and lens. The camera, which was in pristine condition, was worth an estimated £250,000 (over $340,000) on its own! But what made the discovery even more remarkable was that the camera had apparently been hidden in the car by a previous owner who had used it to take secret photos during World War II. Saunders contacted the previous owner's family, who confirmed that their father had indeed been a spy during the war and had used the camera to take pictures of enemy territory. The camera and car were eventually sold at auction for a combined total of £566,000 (over $800,000).

Thank You and we hope you enjoyed our Book.

Please leave us your review.

It will take you only few minutes and it means a lot to us.

Thank You

For more interesting kids books please visit us on Amazon at Medina Press.

Photos Credits:

https://www.flickr.com/photos/4x4paper/
https://www.flickr.com/photos/tomronworldwide/
https://www.flickr.com/photos/micsworld/
https://www.flickr.com/photos/91591049@N00/
https://www.flickr.com/photos/30474136@N07/
https://www.flickr.com/photos/tomsaint/
https://www.flickr.com/photos/greggjerdingen/
https://www.flickr.com/photos/davehamster/